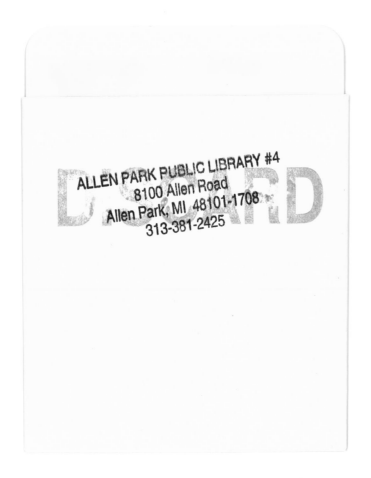

EARLY PEOPLES

THE MAORI

WORLD
BOOK

World Book
a Scott Fetzer company
Chicago
www.worldbookonline.com

World Book, Inc.
233 N. Michigan Avenue
Chicago, IL 60601
U.S.A.

For information about other World Book publications, visit our
Web site at http://www.worldbookonline.com or call
1-800-WORLDBK (967-5325).
For information about sales to schools and libraries, call
1-800-975-3250 (United States), or 1-800-837-5365 (Canada).

Library of Congress Cataloging-in-Publication Data

The Maori.
   p. cm. — (Early peoples)
  Includes index.
  Summary: "A discussion of the Maori, including their history, social
structure, religion, art and architecture, science and technology, daily
life, and entertainment and sports, as well as the decline and
revitalization of the Maori culture. Features include timelines, fact
boxes, glossary, list of recommended reading and web sites, and
index"—Provided by publisher.
  ISBN 978-0-7166-2143-0
  1. Maori (New Zealand people)—History—Juvenile literature.
2. Maori (New Zealand people)—Social life and customs—Juvenile
literature. I. World Book, Inc.
DU423.A1M315 2009
305.89'9442—dc22
                                   2008039327

Printed in China by Leo Paper Products Ltd.,
Heshan, Guangdong
2nd printing June 2010

STAFF

EXECUTIVE COMMITTEE
President
 Paul A. Gazzolo
Vice President and Chief Marketing Officer
 Patricia Ginnis
Vice President and Chief Financial Officer
 Donald D. Keller
Vice President and Editor in Chief
 Paul A. Kobasa
Director, Human Resources
 Bev Ecker
Chief Technology Officer
 Tim Hardy
Managing Director, International
 Benjamin Hinton

EDITORIAL
Editor in Chief
 Paul A. Kobasa
Associate Director, Supplementary
Publications
 Scott Thomas
Managing Editor, Supplementary
Publications
 Barbara A. Mayes
Senior Editor, Supplementary Publications
 Kristina Vaicikonis
Manager, Research, Supplementary
Publications
 Cheryl Graham
Manager, Contracts and Compliance
(Rights and Permissions)
 Loranne K. Shields

Administrative Assistant
 Ethel Matthews
Editors
 Nicholas Kilzer
 Scott Richardson
 Christine Sullivan

GRAPHICS AND DESIGN
Associate Director
 Sandra M. Dyrlund
Manager
 Tom Evans
Coordinator, Design Development and
Production
 Brenda B. Tropinski

EDITORIAL ADMINISTRATION
Director, Systems and Projects
 Tony Tills
Senior Manager, Publishing Operations
 Timothy Falk

PRODUCTION
Director, Manufacturing and Pre-Press
 Carma Fazio
Manufacturing Manager
 Steve Hueppchen
Production/Technology Manager
 Anne Fritzinger
Production Specialist
 Curley Hunter
Proofreader
 Emilie Schrage

MARKETING
Chief Marketing Officer
 Patricia Ginnis
Associate Director, School and Library
Marketing
 Jennifer Parello

Produced for World Book by
 White-Thomson Publishing Ltd.
+44 (0)845 362 8240
www.wtpub.co.uk
Steve White-Thomson, President

Writer: Geoffrey M. Horn
Editor: Kelly Davis
Designer: Simon Borrough
Photo Researcher: Amy Sparks
Map Artist: Stefan Chabluk
Illustrator: Adam Hook (p. 41)
Fact Checker: Charlene Rimsa
Proofreader: Catherine Gardner
Indexer: Nila Glikin

Consultant:
Dr. Nathan Matthews
Lecturer in the School of Maori, Pacific
and Indigenous Studies
University of Otago
New Zealand

TABLE OF CONTENTS

Glossary There is a glossary on pages 60-61. Terms defined in the glossary are in type **that looks like this** on their first appearance on any spread (two facing pages).

Additional Resources Books for further reading and recommended Web sites are listed on page 62. Because of the nature of the Internet, some Web site addresses may have changed since publication. The publisher has no responsibility for any such changes or for the content of cited sources.

WHO ARE THE MAORI?

The original settlers of New Zealand are called Maori *(MAH oh ree or MOW ree)*. Scholars believe Maori first arrived in New Zealand around A.D. 1200. They **migrated** from islands in what is now central Polynesia *(POL uh NEE zhuh)*. Polynesia, which means *many islands,* covers a large area of the central Pacific Ocean.

New Zealand is located in the southwest Pacific. Most of New Zealand's land area consists of two long islands—the North Island and the South Island. New Zealand is famed for its natural beauty. Both of its large islands have steep mountains and lush green lowlands. Maori called New Zealand **Aotearoa** *(ah aw teh ah roh ah)*, which means *the land of the long white cloud.*

◄ A Maori girl, wearing a traditional grass skirt and cape, stands before an intricately carved gateway at Waiotapu, New Zealand.

Maori shared many religious beliefs and social customs with other Polynesian peoples. Chief among these were the belief in **mana** *(MAH nah)* and **tapu** *(tah poo)*, or taboo. Mana was a **supernatural** *(soo puhr NACH uhr uhl)* force connected to gods, spirits, powerful individuals, and special objects. Tapu was the basis of law and behavior in all of Polynesia. Tapu prohibited certain actions, activities, and foods because they were sacred, dangerous, or unclean. In addition, Maori worshiped many gods and spirits.

How Maori Got Their Name

The Polynesians of New Zealand adopted the name Maori in the early 1800's. At that time, white settlers had begun arriving from Europe. Maori called themselves tangata maori *(tahng ah tah mow ree)*, meaning *ordinary person*. The Polynesians called the Europeans **Pakeha** *(PAH keh hah)*, which loosely translates as *foreigner*.

Maori Fall and Rise

Maori were great warriors, and rival Maori groups frequently fought against one another. Maori also fought the Europeans, often over land.

By the end of the 1800's, Europeans had seized most Maori land. In the 1870's, fewer than 50,000 Maori lived in New Zealand. However, new Maori leaders in the early 1900's helped revive their culture and language. Relations between Maori and Pakeha improved. Today, many more Maori live in New Zealand than before the arrival of the Europeans.

NAVIGATORS OF THE PACIFIC

The Maori's ancestors were great voyagers. These Polynesians traveled hundreds of miles across the Pacific Ocean, from island to island, in large double canoes propelled by paddles and sails.

Preparing for the Long Haul

About 2,000 years ago, Polynesian voyagers reached the Society Islands. From there, they began to establish **colonies** on other island groups in the Pacific. Their canoes carried plants, animals, stone tools, and supplies to make a new life in a new land.

Sailing by Double Canoe

To make their double canoes, the Polynesians set two canoe **hulls** side-by-side. Then they connected the two hulls with wooden crossbeams roped to the canoes. A wooden platform was placed on top of the crossbeams. This platform supported tall wooden poles, from which fabric sails were hung. The platform also served as a work, rest, and storage area. A double canoe could be 60 feet (18 meters) or more in length. It was much more stable than a single canoe in rough waters.

▼ An anchor stone from a Maori war canoe, which was found in Poverty Bay, on the east coast of New Zealand's North Island. The carved face design indicates which canoe it was used for.

DIFFERENT CANOES FOR DIFFERENT TASKS

Like their Polynesian ancestors, Maori sometimes built large double-hulled canoes for sailing on ocean waters. More commonly, Maori canoes had single hulls. These were dugout canoes, shaped from a hollowed-out tree trunk. Simple canoes were used to ferry people and goods on lakes and rivers. Fishing canoes were more highly decorated, with fine woodcarvings on the front and back. Most impressive of all were the war canoes. These had richly detailed carvings on the front, back, and sides. On the **prow**, a carved head—perhaps a war god—gazed fiercely at the enemy. Feathers and paint made the war canoe an even more fearsome sight.

When sailing across open seas, how did these brave explorers **navigate?** They had no instruments to help them find their way. Landmarks were few and far between. Instead, the Polynesian voyagers relied on observing the positions of the sun, moon, and stars to guide their boats. They also carefully noted the movement of ocean waves and currents, as well as the paths of birds flying overhead.

▼ A depiction of a Maori war canoe by George French Angas, a British painter. Angas traveled in New Zealand in 1844 and made many pencil sketches of Maori. These sketches were the basis for a volume of hand-colored prints, *The New Zealanders Illustrated*, published in 1847.

HOW DO WE KNOW ABOUT MAORI HISTORY?

The earliest written accounts of Maori life and history come from European **missionaries** *(MIHSH uh nehr eez)*. These visitors did not understand the Polynesians' way of life and often did not approve of the Polynesians' religious beliefs. As a result, the writings can be misleading.

Before the arrival of the Europeans, Maori had no written language. Stories and legends were passed down by word of mouth from generation to generation. Europeans taught Maori how to write, at which point Maori began recording their own history.

Kupe's Voyage

Maori tradition says the first Polynesian man to travel by canoe to New Zealand was Kupe *(koo pay)*. He came from **Hawaiki** *(ha wa EE kee)*, the legendary Polynesian homeland.

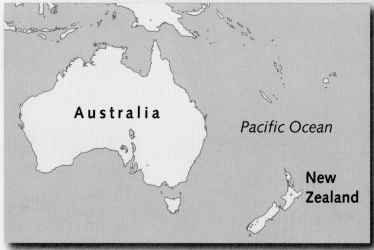

▼ New Zealand is located southeast of Australia. The country has two main islands, the North Island and the South Island, as well as several smaller islands.

According to one story, Kupe left Hawaiki in pursuit of a giant octopus. He chased the octopus all the way to the passage separating the North Island from the South Island, now known as Cook Strait. There, Kupe finally caught the monstrous creature and killed it. According to tradition, Kupe was the first to use the name **Aotearoa** to describe the land. He is also credited with naming many other places in New Zealand.

▲ Rock carvings, thought to be around 700 years old, may represent the canoes that brought Maori ancestors to New Zealand. These carvings are located in the Kaingaroa caves, in South Auckland, on the North Island. At the base of the wall is a discarded Maori canoe.

Archaeological Evidence

Although **archaeologists** *(AHR kee OL uh jihstz)* cannot be sure if Kupe was a historical figure, they do know that Polynesians were expert navigators who traveled long distances. Polynesians took dogs, pigs, and chickens with them in their canoes. The canoes also carried rats. Archaeologists don't know whether the rats were deliberately brought as food or came aboard as stowaways.

Remains of the Pacific rat have been found on many islands. By studying their **DNA**, scientists have learned a great deal about where and when the Polynesians traveled. (DNA is a molecule found in every living thing that determines an organism's characteristics.) Analysis of rat DNA supports the idea that New Zealand was settled as the result of several different canoe voyages. These canoes may have come from different Pacific islands at different times.

The Polynesians may have sailed as far east as South America. Some experts believe that **kumara** *(koo mah rah)*, a kind of sweet potato that Polynesians brought to New Zealand, originated in South America.

MAORI SOCIETY

The story of Kupe did not end with his arrival in **Aotearoa**. According to **legend**, Kupe returned to **Hawaiki** and told the people there of his discovery. He said the new land was beautiful, and there was plenty of food. Later, when a war broke out on Hawaiki, some Polynesians decided to leave their homeland. They launched their canoes and sailed to the land that Kupe had described.

Tribes, Clans, and Families

This fleet of canoes held members of different tribes, each led by a paramount chief, or **ariki** *(ah ree kee)*. When the canoes landed in New Zealand, more than 40 tribes, or **iwi** *(ee wee)*, spread out to settle the country. Most settled on the North Island, which was warmer and better suited for growing crops. A few tribes settled the northern part of the South Island.

TREASURED POSSESSIONS

The most valuable Maori treasures were **taonga** *(tah on gah)*. A taonga could be a skill, such as the ability to carve a canoe. Or it could be an object, such as the weapon of a famous warrior. Famous weapons were given names, such as "Man-Eater" or "Forest of Blood." To be given such a weapon—or to capture it on the battlefield—was a great honor.

Such **ornaments** as necklaces and hair combs were also taonga. Maori believed that an ornament passed down from chief to chief contained some of the **mana** of each chief who wore it. Contact with taonga connected each member of a tribe with his or her ancestors. The taonga allowed Maori to feel that their ancestors were actually present among them.

▲ A chief's precious ceremonial **adz** (a tool used for smoothing rough-cut wood) dates from the 1800's. The wooden handle was a symbol of the chief who owned it and would have been buried with him. The blade, made of a kind of **jade** called greenstone, would have been given to the next chief. He would have attached it to a new handle.

▲ A man's cloak made of fine **flax** fibers woven using the fingers and decorated with lengths of flax dyed black.

Before the Europeans came, Maori did not think of themselves as Maori. They saw themselves as part of an iwi. Each iwi included several **clans,** or **hapu** *(ha poo)*. Finally, each clan might include several large or extended families. These were known as **whanau** *(fah now)*. Each person's social position was largely defined by the whanau, hapu, and iwi to which he or she belonged.

From Generation to Generation

Maori believed that everything came from something else. Their word for this idea was **whakapapa** *(fah kah pah pah)*. Everything had a whakapapa—gods, people, animals, even trees and rocks.

All Maori parents were expected to teach the names of their immediate ancestors to their children. Each tribe had **elders** who knew the names of all the tribes' ancestors. The tribal history extended all the way back to the name of the chief who had made the journey from Hawaiki.

THE POWER OF THE CHIEFS

At the head of each **iwi** (tribe) was an **ariki** (paramount chief). The ariki held the highest rank in Maori society. Each ariki was a living link with the original chiefs who had sailed from **Hawaiki**. Only the gods had more power than the arikis.

Each ariki might have more than one wife, and each wife might have several children. The title of ariki normally passed from the paramount chief to his first-born son. If the first child was a girl, she might grow up to hold a position of great honor. But girls rarely held the title of ariki.

Role of the Ariki

The title of ariki carried great privilege and respect. The ariki could declare war or make peace. He conducted negotiations with other tribes. He settled disputes between rival **clans.** He had authority over the iwi's land and all the activities that took place on it. His household claimed a share of whatever the iwi's farmers, hunters, and fishers produced.

The ariki was not a dictator, however. In tribal councils, all **hapu,** or clan, leaders could speak their minds.

◀ An 1890 depiction of the Maori warrior and chief Tamati Waka Nene. The oil-on-canvas portrait was painted by the Bohemian-born artist Gottfried Lindauer.

Clan Leaders

Much of the real power in Maori society was held by clan leaders. In fact, hapu leaders had more say than the ariki over how people lived their daily lives. The chief of each hapu commanded the fighters who defended the clan and its lands. The chief was also responsible for making sure the hapu stored enough food to get through difficult times.

The chief of each hapu held the title of **rangatira** *(rang ah tee rah)*. The rules about who could become rangatira varied from iwi to iwi and from hapu to hapu. In some clans, the leader received his title from his father. In others, the selection was based on merit. For example, a great warrior might become a rangatira. Women held the title in some clans.

A GIRL AS CHIEF?

The 2002 movie *Whale Rider* (below) was a worldwide hit. Although the film is set in modern New Zealand, it draws on Maori **legends** and customs. In the movie, a Maori girl named Paikea, played by Keisha Castle-Hughes, comes from a long line of chiefs. But her grandfather, Koro—the current chief— thinks only a first-born son is fit to be a leader. Paikea sets out to prove her grandfather wrong.

FIERCE WARRIORS

War was a major part of Maori life. **Archaeologists** have found the remains of nearly 7,000 **fortified** Maori villages, or **pa** *(pah)*. Typically, a pa was protected by a complex system of fences, watchtowers, ditches, and earthen barriers. The first pa were probably built around 1500; the last, in 1881.

Boys were taught to fight from an early age. Women also could be warriors. They were expected to defend their homes and children from attack. Sometimes they joined—or led—war parties that attacked rival **clans.**

Wars between clans were rarely fought for land or conquest. More often, they were fought as revenge for some harm or insult committed by members of one clan against another.

▼ The overgrown ruins of a pa on the North Island.

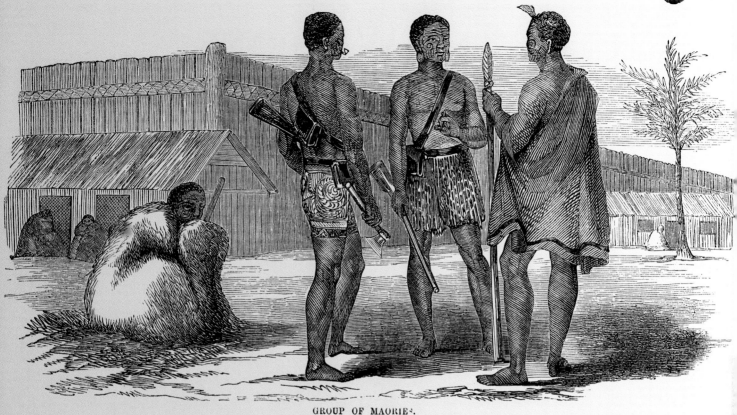

GROUP OF MAORIES.

▲ An engraving from the mid-1850's depicting Maori warriors armed with spears, hatchets, and rifles. The wooden fence surrounding their pa can be seen in the background.

EATING THE ENEMY
Maori worshiped the war god, Tu *(too)*. Maori myths told of how Tu took revenge on his enemies and ate their children. Like Tu, Maori ate some of their enemies. This practice has been explained in several ways. The most likely reason is that by eating the enemy, the warrior hoped to gain some of the fallen fighter's power, or **mana**.

A Season for Fighting

Most wars were fought between November and April, during the New Zealand summer. The season for war began after the main planting was finished. It ended when the clan had to finish the harvest and prepare for winter. Summer had several advantages as a time for battle. War parties could travel farther during the long days of summer. Because fish and wild animals were plentiful during that season, the warriors had a ready supply of food while on the move.

Preparing for War

Before taking military action, a **rangatira** (clan leader) had to make sure the **hapu** was ready for war. An assembly was held, in which speeches, songs, and chants strengthened the clan's fighting spirit.

Normally, each hapu had about 70 fighters. If an enemy appeared to be much stronger, the rangatira might appeal for help. For example, the chief might send a gift, such as a burnt cloak, as a kind of coded message to the rangatira of a friendly clan. If the clan leader accepted the gift, its fighters would join the war party.

TACTICS AND WEAPONS

A surprise attack was the chief Maori battle tactic. No village could afford to let down its guard. According to a Maori saying, "Birds sleep soundly and peacefully on a tree branch. But man is ever wakeful and in dread of enemies."

Types of Battles

Most often, attackers would advance at night, their movements hidden by forests, mist, and rain. Anyone the fighters met on the way would be killed. At dawn, the attackers would strike, hoping to catch the enemy unprepared.

Many battles were quick. But an attack on a fortified village, or **pa**, might take much longer. Some battles were decided by hand-to-hand combat between the leading warrior on each side.

If the battle went well, the attackers might take some women and children back to their home village as slaves. The enemy warriors would be killed—and perhaps eaten.

Clubs and Other Weapons

Before Europeans came, Maori fought mainly with clubs. The long club was made of wood or, less often, of whalebone. It measured from 5 to 9 feet (1.5 to 2.7 meters) and was held with two hands. The head of the club could be decorated and shaped in various ways. For example, a type of club called a tewhatewha *(teh fah teh fah)* had feathers and a head shaped like an axe.

◀ A short wooden club, made in the 1700's and used by Maori warriors for thrusting and parrying when fighting at close quarters.

The long club was used for thrusting and slashing, to keep the enemy at a distance. If that failed and the enemy came closer, warriors switched to the short club. Short clubs were swung with one hand. They were commonly made of stone, wood, or whalebone. A great warrior might wield a club carved from greenstone, a form of **jade**.

Another Maori weapon was the kotaha *(koh tah hah)*, a kind of slingshot. It was used to shoot darts or fiery objects at the enemy. After the Europeans came, the Maori traded with them to get **muskets** and gunpowder.

▶ A portrait of a tattooed Maori warrior, by the New Zealand artist Charles Frederick Goldie.

Maori Women and Men

In some ways, Maori women and men were equals. Girls were taught how to defend themselves if their village was attacked. Women fought alongside men to defend their homes. In a few tribes, women commanded bands of warriors.

One area in which women excelled was the creative arts. Women wrote songs and chants, or **haka** *(HAH kah)*, of all kinds. These haka were performed by both women and men.

Marriage and Children

In many areas of daily life, women and men followed different roles and rules. Women were expected to produce children. If a woman did not have a child, her husband might divorce her. Or he might take an additional wife to bear his children.

Multiple marriages were much more common among men than among women. But some Maori histories recall high-ranking women who had more than one husband at the same time.

WOMEN AS SPEECH MAKERS

When an assembly was held, women as well as men gave speeches. In the Arawa *(ah rah wah)* area of the North Island, elderly women felt free to comment on each speaker. They would judge how well the speaker did and call out corrections if the speaker made any errors.

◀ Maori women in a **pa** braid **flax** for baskets, in a photograph from the early 1900's. In the background, another woman can be seen weaving a flax robe. The fabric is stretched between two upright sticks.

Daily Tasks, Different Roles

Men did most of the outside work that demanded physical strength. Such tasks included cutting down trees and preparing land for planting crops. Men also did many of the jobs that involved daring or danger. Women tended to do such common household tasks as carrying water, gathering firewood, and collecting berries.

Men dug up fern roots for food, but women carried the roots back to the village. Men took canoes out on the ocean to catch fish; women collected shellfish along the shore. Men trapped birds and small animals; women cooked and preserved foods for storage.

Women as well as men worked with fibers. But they often created different things. Women usually wove cloaks, mats, and baskets. Men were more likely to make ropes and nets. Men used these woven objects in hunting, fishing, and canoe building.

Some jobs were forbidden to women. For example, only men were allowed to carve wood and make canoes.

▲ Maori men paddle a traditional war canoe before the first race of the 2000 America's Cup yacht competition, held in New Zealand.

SPECIALISTS AND THEIR SKILLS

Maori society recognized people with special knowledge and skills. Such people were called **tohunga** *(toh hoong ah)*, which means *experts*. There were different kinds of tohunga. Some were priests; others were healers.

Scholars and teachers learned chants and prayers. They also knew about tribal ancestors, the movements of the stars in the heavens, and other subjects. Their main task was to keep Maori history and traditions alive.

Someone with special knowledge or training in carving or canoe building was also regarded as a tohunga. Other tohunga specialized in tattooing or in helping women give birth. Most tohunga came from families of high rank.

Woodcarvers

Maori thought of woodcarving as a **sacred** activity. Only men were allowed to take part. In many tribes, women were not even allowed to enter a place where wood was being carved. Cooked food was also barred from any place where carvings were made.

▶ A wooden carving, dating from the 1700's, that originally stood before a Maori store-house. The carving depicts two Maori gods, Ranginui *(rang ee noo ee)* the sky father and Papatuanuku *(pah pah too ah noo koo)* the earth mother.

Woodcarvings adorned Maori homes and meeting houses. Every war canoe had detailed carvings in front and back and on the sides. Smaller objects such as treasure boxes were also carved from wood. Craftsmen carved humanlike figures of gods and ancestors as well.

Tools of the Trade

For many of their carvings the Maori used the wood of the kauri *(KOW ree)* and totara *(TOH tuhr uh)* trees. Both grew to heights of more than 82 feet (25 meters). A large dugout canoe could be carved from a single kauri or totara.

JADE JEWELRY

Maori carvers used jade to create hei tiki *(heh ee tee kee)*, which were worn as neck **ornaments**. A hei tiki looked like a small person—often a woman—sitting with crossed legs and large head tilted to the side. Maori believed that the ornaments might help women become pregnant. Maori lore told of childless women who were given hei tiki by their husbands or parents and later had children.

Before the Europeans came, Maori had no metal tools. They made hammers of wood or whalebone. Carving tools were fashioned from stone. A form of **jade** called nephrite *(NEHF ryt)* was especially good for carving wood. This hard mineral, which Maori called pounamu *(poh oo nah moo)*, is found only on the South Island. It is also known as greenstone or New Zealand jade. Maori also used greenstone in jewelry.

▶ An unusually large hei tiki or breast **pendant** measures about 6 inches (16 centimeters) in length. Hei tiki were prized as personal ornaments. Some hei tiki also became sacred clan possessions that were passed down for many generations.

PRISONERS AND SLAVES

An elderly slave woman wrapped in a **flax** cloak squats in front of a **pa** fence (top, center) in a page from the sketchbook of British artist George French Angas, dated 1844. Also shown are two elaborately carved canoe paddles (on either side), a young child (bottom, center), and a carved club with a feathered handle (bottom, right).

Maori captured few prisoners in battle. Most of those who were allowed to live were women and children. They were taken as slaves.

Slaves occupied the lowest rung on the Maori social ladder. Slavery was a mark of shame. A slave who escaped and returned to his or her **hapu** might be treated as an outcast.

Treatment of Slaves

Slaves were regarded as property. Often they became part of the **rangatira's** household. In theory, the chief had complete power over them. The clan leader could decide whether a slave lived or died.

In practice, however, slaves could be well treated. They were allowed to do anything that was **noa** *(noh ah)*, a Maori word that means *ordinary* or *commonplace*. Many of the chores Maori women did were also noa. For this reason, high-born women let their slaves take over many of the routine tasks involved in running a household.

Slaves were not allowed to perform tasks that had special rules or status, such as carving and canoe building. But slaves were allowed to paddle canoes and assist when the rangatira went to war.

Sometimes a free Maori of low rank would marry a slave. Any child born to that couple was regarded as free. But the child was also likely to hold a low rank in society. In addition, the stain of slavery might continue for generations. Having an ancestor who had been a slave was a bad mark for any Maori.

European Influences

The coming of Europeans had an unexpected impact on slavery. Traditional Maori weapons and tactics emphasized hand-to-hand combat. This did not make it easy to control large numbers of captives. But **muskets**—brought to New Zealand by the **Pakeha**—made the taking of prisoners much less difficult. For this reason, slavery actually increased in the decades following European contact.

European Christians strongly disapproved of both slavery and cannibalism, however. As Christianity spread among the Maori, both practices died out.

THE MORIORI

A different group of Polynesians, called the Moriori *(MOH ree OH ree)*, settled what are now New Zealand's Chatham Islands at about the same time that Maori settled the mainland. The Chatham Islands group is about 530 miles (850 kilometers) east of the South Island.

In the late 1700's, more than 1,000 Moriori lived in the Chathams. In the 1830's, Maori warriors invaded the islands. They killed and ate many Moriori and took nearly all the rest as slaves. By 1840, fewer than 100 Moriori were left. The 1901 census found only 35 Moriori in New Zealand. By 2006, however, their number had increased to 945.

▼ A carved wooden box that held the body of a slave who rose to become a chief in the Northland region (the northernmost tip of the North Island). When a high-ranking Maori died, the body was left on a raised platform until the flesh rotted away. The bones were then cleaned, painted red, and put into a box, which was placed inside a cave.

LAW AND ORDER

Maori did not have a formal justice system. There were no police, no lawyers, no courts, and no jails. But Maori did have a clear sense of right and wrong. Disputes were resolved by applying two basic ideas: **utu** *(oo too)* and **muru** *(moo roo)*.

Utu—The Need for Balance

The basic idea behind utu was balance. In some cases, this involved revenge. Any injury had to be answered. If someone was killed—even by accident—members of the dead person's **clan** had a right to take revenge. Members of the killer's clan understood and accepted that right.

Utu also involved balance in other forms. For example, if one Maori chief gave another chief a gift, the second chief was expected to return a gift of equal or greater value. This gift did not have to be given immediately. It might be repaid months or even years later. It might even be repaid by another generation—for example, by the second chief's grandchild or great-grandchild.

In the same way, if someone showed kindness to someone else, that kindness needed to be repaid. A failure to give or receive utu reflected badly on both sides. It also reflected badly on the group—the **whanau** or **hapu**—to which the individuals belonged.

MURU AND A GARDEN HOE

The idea of muru continued to shape Maori thought even after Christian **missionaries** arrived from Europe. A Maori named Polack had a servant who accidentally threw a garden hoe that hit the leg of a chief. The chief complained loudly, and it was agreed that a muru was required. The following Sunday, the chief sent one of his slaves to Polack. The slave told Polack that the chief did not want to upset the missionaries by carrying out the muru raid on a Sunday. Would it be all right, the slave asked, if the raiding party came to take Polack's property on Monday instead?

▲ A sketch of a muru, dated between 1860 and 1890, by an unknown Maori artist. Muru was a form of justice under which the clan of a person who was harmed could, under certain conditions, take property from the clan of the person held responsible for the harm.

Muru—Taking Someone Else's Property

Under certain conditions, a Maori who was wronged was allowed to take some of the wrongdoer's property. This form of justice was called muru. The wrongdoer was not expected to resist.

The idea of muru applied to groups as well as to individuals. When someone was harmed in some way, members of that person's clan would meet to discuss whether a muru raid was called for. At the meeting, clan members would decide how many people would take part in the raid and how much would be taken. Sometimes the wronged clan and the clan that had done the wrong worked out the terms of the muru in advance.

RELIGIOUS BELIEFS

The Maori view of life was shaped by the daily pattern of sunrise and sunset. Each day at dawn, the sun was born out of darkness. As the sun rose higher and higher in the sky, the amount of light and energy in the world increased. But as evening neared, the sun grew weary, and its light and energy became weaker. Each night the sun died, only to be reborn the following day.

▼ A flat wooden treasure box, used to hold **ornaments** that had been worn on a chief's head and were therefore tapu, or taboo. Such a treasure box would be hung high in the rafters of the house, so that the residents were not endangered by contact with its powerful contents.

PRESERVING THE HEAD

Maori believed that a person's head contained much of his or her mana, or power. Anything that touched the head of a chief (or someone else of high rank) was tapu. There were strict rules for how to handle a comb or earrings—even hair clippings.

When a chief died, his head might be cut off and preserved. In that way, the **clan** and family could continue to share the chief's mana. The preserved head would then become a **taonga**, or treasured possession.

How the World Began

Maori believed that the world began as Te Kore *(teh koh ray)*. Te Kore is sometimes translated into English as *nothingness*. But the Maori idea was much richer than that. For Maori, Te Kore was formless, but it was filled with possibilities.

Te Kore was not dark or light. It was not male or female. But it had the potential to become all those things, and many more. What gave each of these things its special nature was the **mauri** *(mah oo ree)*, or life force. The Maori believed that everything—rivers, trees, birds, fish, people—had its own particular mauri. Mauri came from the actions of the gods.

Tapu—Handle with Care

Maori life was governed by the idea of **tapu,** which means *set apart*. In theory, anything could be tapu, because everything was created by the gods. Tapu was closely related to the idea of **mana.** Because all things shared the mana of the gods, they could be dangerous if not handled properly.

Maori had ways of turning things that were tapu into things that were **noa**, or commonplace. For example, a newly built house was tapu. It was therefore dangerous for ordinary people to enter. But after a **ritual** in which a high-born woman entered the house, it was considered noa and so was safe for people of lower rank to follow.

▲ A Maori knife, carved from wood, decorated with shells, and edged with shark's teeth. This kind of knife was used only for cutting human flesh—a dangerous and tapu task.

CREATION STORIES

Maori beliefs about creation differed from **iwi** to iwi. But they all attempted to explain how the natural world came to exist.

Sky Father and Earth Mother

In Maori tradition, the world's two parents were Ranginui and Papatuanuku. Ranginui is the sky father. Papatuanuku is the earth mother. From her, all things are born.

▲ An ancient stone statue of a fertility god. Maori tradition holds that this statue was brought from the legendary Maori homeland of **Hawaiki.** It stands on Mokoia Island.

▲ A wooden carving from the mid-1800's that once decorated the entrance to a house. The carving depicts the separation of the two most important Maori gods, Ranginui the sky father and Papatuanuku the earth mother.

Ranginui and Papatuanuku embraced very tightly, leaving only darkness between them. Into that darkness, a number of gods were born. Two of these gods were Tu, the god of war, and Tane *(tah nay)*, the god of the forests. Other gods ruled the seas, the weather, earthquakes, farming, and the world of darkness and evil.

Raising the Sky

Many stories were told about Tane, the forest god. Tane and the other gods grew up in the darkness between their parents. As they got older, the gods tried to separate their father from their mother, so the light of life could enter the world. The war god Tu tried but failed. Tangaroa *(tan gah roh ah)*, god of the seas, was also unsuccessful.

Finally Tane tried. He lay on his back—some versions of the **myth** say he stood on his head—and pushed his father and mother apart, while the other gods helped. Then he planted wooden posts in the ground, so the sky would remain above the earth. Maori tradition also held that Tane made the first woman out of clay. He was regarded as the father of humanity.

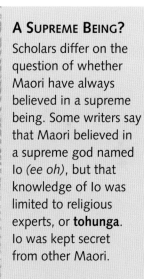

A SUPREME BEING?

Scholars differ on the question of whether Maori have always believed in a supreme being. Some writers say that Maori believed in a supreme god named Io *(ee oh)*, but that knowledge of Io was limited to religious experts, or **tohunga**. Io was kept secret from other Maori.

Other scholars say that belief in Io did not develop until the 1800's, after European **missionaries** came. According to this view, Maori started to believe in Io after they learned Christian ideas about God.

RITUALS OF LIFE AND DEATH

Many **rituals** took place on the village **marae** *(muh RY)*, a large open area next to the community meeting house. One important ritual was the **powhiri** *(poh fee ree)*, a ceremony of welcome. Another was the funeral, or **tangihanga** *(tang ee hang ah)*.

Welcoming Visitors

Each tribe and **clan** had different customs for the powhiri. But each welcoming ceremony on the marae was likely to begin with a challenge. One of the strongest warriors in the village would place a dart or other object on the ground in front of the visitors. If the visitor picked up the item while keeping his or her eyes on the warrior, this proved the visitor had come in peace.

▼ Two Maori women press their noses together in a traditional greeting called a hongi, in a photograph taken on the North Island.

TREATING ILLNESS

Maori believed that sickness was caused by evil spirits. Evil spirits could enter a person's body if the laws of **tapu** were broken. The laws might have been broken by the patient (perhaps by accident) or by someone who wanted to harm the patient.

When a Maori became sick, a healer would be called. This healer was an expert, or **tohunga.** The tohunga would try to get rid of the evil spirits through prayers and spells. The tohunga might also know some plants that could help the patient feel better.

The next part of the powhiri ceremony was the women's call, which was followed by a dance of welcome, formal speeches, and a chant. The visitors would then offer a gift to the hosts. Traditionally, the gift was a precious object, perhaps a cloak or a carving made of greenstone or whalebone.

After the gift was accepted, the hosts and guests shared a traditional Maori greeting—the **hongi** *(hong ee)*. In the hongi, one Maori gently pressed his or her nose against another's. The powhiri ended with the hosts and guests sharing a feast.

Saying Farewell to the Dead

The Maori word for funeral—*tangihanga*—includes the word *tangi*, which means *to cry* or *to mourn.* Typically, a funeral lasted for at least three days. During that period, members of the extended family talked to and about the dead person. There was speechmaking and singing. The mourners would go without food during the day, then feast at night. At least one family member stayed with the body the whole time.

As with the ceremony of welcome, the women's call was an important part of the ritual. At the funeral, the women would hold leaves in their hands. The leaves were gently waved from left to right, to ease the dead person's path into the spirit world. Relatives might shade their eyes with leaves to allow them to see the dead person's spirit.

▶ A carved stone statue called a **mauri** stone was sometimes placed in a forest to protect the plants and animals living there. Maori believed that such stones concentrated the forest's mauri, the force that gave life to all living things.

MAORI ARTS AND CRAFTS

Maori arts reflected the religious and cultural beliefs of these Polynesian people. Wood-carvings of the heads of chiefs and warriors were not just beautiful designs. They were meant to summon up the power of the ancestors. Pieces made of whalebone and greenstone were not just items in a collection. They were **taonga**—treasures that held the **mana** of those who had possessed them.

Carving Styles

Maori woodcarving styles changed over the centuries. The earliest carvings were similar to those of other Polynesian peoples. Later carvings showed major differences from place to place and tribe to tribe.

We know about some of the earliest carvings because Maori believed the carvings might be dangerous if they fell into enemy hands. Maori kept these carvings safe

▲ An early Maori rock drawing, dated around 1400, of a fish with several birdlike figures. The drawing indicates the importance of fishing and hunting as food sources for Maori people.

BASKETS FOR ALL PURPOSES
Maori used flax to make many kinds of baskets, or **kete** *(keh teh)*. One kind of basket was used for gathering shellfish, another for harvesting **kumara**. Separate kinds of kete were made for serving food and for squeezing juice from berries. In general, women and slaves carried baskets on their backs. Warriors and high-ranking men slung their kete over one shoulder.

by hiding them in swamps. The oldest surviving Maori carving was found near Kaitaia, in the far north region of the North Island. It is between 700 and 900 years old.

The Kaitaia carving may have been the top of a gateway. In the center, it shows a front view of a **tiki**, a humanlike figure. On either side, it shows side views of birdlike figures with arms and legs. Whales and sea monsters of various kinds also appear often in Maori woodcarvings.

Fabrics from Flax

Maori weaving and other fiber arts also had Polynesian roots. In their tropical homeland, the Polynesians had made cloth from the paper mulberry tree. But this fabric was not heavy enough for the colder New Zealand climate. There the Polynesians found a new material—a form of **flax** that Maori called harakeke *(hah rah keh keh)*. This plant grew wild in great quantities in wetland areas.

Maori used many kinds of *harakeke* leaves. Some leaves yielded rough, tough fibers that were suitable for ropes, traps, mats, and baskets. Other varieties yielded silky fibers that were perfect for making cloaks. Patterns were added by using dyes extracted from the bark of different trees.

◀ Maori wood-carvers lavished their skills on these five wooden panels, taken from a storehouse and dating from the 1800's. These panels depict the ancestry of the **clan** and the world of the **supernatural**.

BODY ART

Maori were highly skilled at tattooing, which they called **ta moko** *(tah moh koh)*. Tattooing was a form of art that used the face and body as a canvas. The earliest Polynesian settlers of **Aotearoa** brought ta moko with them from their homeland. **Archaeologists** have found tools for ta moko at early New Zealand settlements.

Generally, men received more **moko** than women. Tattoos often covered a man's entire face. Men were also tattooed on the middle and lower body, both front and back. Women most often had tattoos on their chins and upper lips.

▼ A modern Maori man displays a traditional moko.

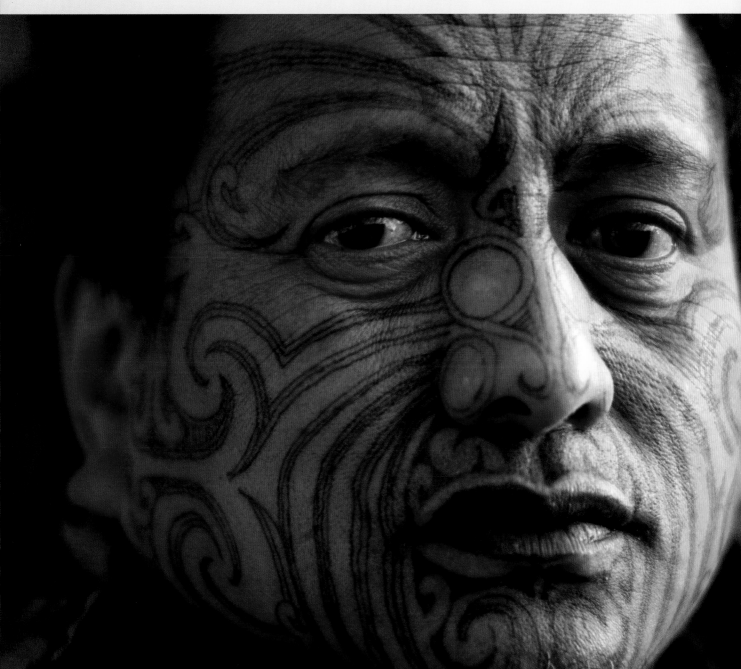

Carving the Face

Getting a full-face moko was a long and painful process. Special tools were used to pierce the skin, cut lines in the face, and press colors into the grooves. The colors—mainly black mixed with different amounts of blue or green—were created by mixing soot with fish oil or animal oil and water. Leaves of the karaka tree were then placed on the cuts to help the skin heal.

Strict **tapu** governed everything about ta moko. The person receiving a full-face moko was not allowed to eat. Instead, he was fed broth and water through a carved funnel.

Understanding Moko

Spiral and leaflike patterns were common in ta moko design. But a facial moko was more than just a fashion statement. A full-face moko was intended to make a warrior look terrifying to an enemy fighter. Designs in particular areas of the face would also convey the wearer's rank in the **hapu**. For a woman, moko around the lips and chin meant that she was old enough to have her words respected by the adult community.

▼ A carved wooden feeding funnel, dating from the 1800's. This funnel was used to prevent food from touching a chief's lips while he was being tattooed. Maori believed that any contact with food before the moko had healed would destroy their spiritual power.

A EUROPEAN VIEW OF MOKO

Sir Joseph Banks was among the first Europeans to visit New Zealand. He sailed with Captain James Cook on the H.M.S. *Endeavour*, which reached New Zealand in 1769. Banks was stunned by the beauty and variety of Maori ta moko. He wrote: "It was impossible to avoid admiring the immense Elegance and Justness of the figures in which it is form'd … all these finish'd with a masterly taste and execution, for of a hundred which at first sight you would judge to be exactly the same, on a close examination, no two will prove alike."

THE MARAE

The **marae** was the heart of Maori village life. It was a large open area where people met for war councils, weddings, funerals, and other community events. The marae was also used for informal meetings. It was a place where people could gather in the sunshine to eat, play, and chat.

Traditionally, the marae was an open space in front of a meeting house or the home of a chief. In time, however, the word was applied to any large community space, including the meeting house and other buildings.

◄ The grand entrance to a Maori meeting house. To the left of the doorway is the structure's intricately carved main supporting post. On the right side is a self-portrait of the chief carver.

The Carved Meeting House

Over the centuries, the meeting house next to the open area became increasingly important as a community center. The most beautiful Maori buildings were carved meeting houses. The Maori name for these was **whare whakairo** *(fah ray fah ky roh)*. The oldest surviving whare whakairo dates from 1842.

The typical meeting house was about 33 feet (10 meters) long. Tall wooden poles in front and back supported a long, steeply angled roof. At the top of the roof, extending from front to back, was the beautifully carved ridge-pole, or tahuhu *(tah hoo hoo)*. Inside the meeting house, one or more poles—also wonderfully carved—supported the tahuhu.

Speaking to Ancestors

For Maori, the carved meeting house was not merely a wooden building. It was a tribute to former chiefs and their ancestors. Their images decorated the support poles. The meeting house might be named for a particularly powerful ancestor. The tahuhu was thought to be his backbone, and the boards holding up the roof represented his ribs.

Maori were great speechmakers. They directed their words to **clan** members in the marae. But they also addressed their speeches to the ancestors in the meeting house. They spoke to the meeting house as if it, too, were alive.

▲ A Maori man wears a ceremonial cloak and carries a ceremonial weapon at Rongopai Marae on the North Island.

FAMILY LIFE

The **whanau**, or extended family, was a basic unit of Maori society. From birth to death, Maori were surrounded by family members. Within the whanau, every Maori (except for slaves) was related to every other Maori by birth or marriage.

▲ Maori children and young adults, photographed in the early 1900's in Rotorua, on the North Island.

Love and Marriage

Young people were expected to fall in love. But especially among higher-ranking families, young love rarely led to marriage. Instead, marriages between young people were arranged by family **elders**. Among **clan** leaders and others of high rank, marriages might be arranged even before children were able to walk. These marriages were seen as ways to strengthen ties between one family or clan and another.

The Story of Hinemoa and Tutanekai

A popular Maori story showed how true love could sometimes triumph over family pressures. Hinemoa was the beautiful daughter of a powerful chief. Many fine young men wanted to marry her. One of these was Tutanekai. He came from a good family. But because his family ranked well below Hinemoa's, he was sure her father would never approve the match.

After a long while, Tutanekai got up the courage to declare his love to Hinemoa. He was thrilled when she told him she loved him, too. He urged her to leave her home and come live with him in his village. "At night," he told her, "listen for the sound of the flute. When you hear it, take a canoe and cross the waters of Lake Rotorua. I will be waiting for you."

Night after night, Tutanekai played his flute, but Hinemoa did not come. Her family, suspecting she might try to leave, had dragged all the canoes far up on shore. The night was dark. The lake was wide. The water was cold. How could she get to Tutanekai? After many nights of crying, Hinemoa had an idea. She tied six hollow **gourds** together to help her stay afloat on the water. Supported by the gourds, she swam across the lake, and the two young lovers were married.

When a couple was old enough to marry, the bride's family went with her to the household where the husband lived. Each family would give gifts to the other. Then the two families would share a meal. After the young couple married, they would often live in the husband's father's house.

Giving Birth

The **tapu** connected with giving birth was very strong. There were no hospitals, and women did not give birth at home. Instead, the birth might take place in a temporary shelter. After the baby was born, the shelter was destroyed.

Special songs were sung during and after the birth. These songs described the great deeds the baby's ancestors had achieved.

▶ A wooden carving depicts a chief holding his two young sons.

Maori Settlements

Maori lived in two main kinds of settlements. The first was the **pa**, a **fortified** village designed to provide a strong defense against enemy attack. The second was the **kainga** *(ky ngah)*, which was not fortified. Every large settlement of either kind had an open-air meeting place, or **marae**.

Pa and Kainga

Many pa were built in areas where nature also provided protection from attackers and storms. Pa were often located in parts of northern New Zealand where winters were mild and summers were long. They were probably designed for year-round living.

The kainga lacked the fences and other forms of protection that made the pa so difficult to attack. In general, kainga were smaller than pa. Some may have been intended for temporary use. A small kainga might have up to four wooden houses, used mostly for sleeping. Other structures included storage pits, a trash dump, and a shelter for cooking.

▼ A rare example of a Maori stone-built storehouse. The storehouse was buried in ash during the 1886 eruption of Mount Tarawera, New Zealand's greatest natural disaster. The structure is now part of the Buried Village, a historic site near Rotorua on the North Island.

Food was cooked in an earth-oven. The oven consisted of an earthen pit in which firewood and stones were placed. The fire burned long enough to heat the stones. The hot stones were then sprinkled with water. A layer of leaves was added, followed by fish, meats, and vegetables. The oven was then covered with more stones and earth, and the food was steamed until done.

▲ Because war was a common part of Maori life, most Maori lived in a pa, a settlement fortified with fences, watchtowers, ditches, and earthen barriers.

Styles of Houses

Early Maori houses were round or oval, like those elsewhere in Polynesia. Rectangular houses may have appeared in New Zealand as early as the 1300's. Houses were usually small, no more than 10 feet (3 meters) long and 6 feet (2 meters) across. At the front were a porch, doorway, and window. To protect its inhabitants from the cold, Maori houses had a sunken floor. This was covered with woven floor mats. Earth piled up against the outside walls of the house offered further protection from wintry weather. Posts supporting the walls and roof were sunk deep into the ground to make the house stable.

CLOTHING AND ADORNMENT

Basic Maori garments were made from **flax** fiber and leaves. Both men and women wore a kilt or loincloth around the waist and a rain cape around the shoulders. When walking on rough or cold ground, they might wear sandals woven from flax or the leaves of the cabbage tree. When fighting a battle or doing heavy work, men might take off all their clothes, leaving themselves uncovered except for their tattoos.

Some women wore a garment called a *tu*, which was a belt with a cord fringe extending from the waist to the knees. The Europeans who came to New Zealand in the 1760's saw women wearing this garment. Captain Cook observed that the women wore a capelike piece of cloth over their shoulders.

▲ A pair of chevron (v-shaped) pendants made of whale ivory from the South Island.

Cloaks with Class

A person's cloak reflected his or her standing in Maori society. Ordinary cloaks were made from flax. Fancier cloaks might have colored borders. Even more elegant garments were made from the skin and hair of dogs. Women also wore cloaks, though these were usually plainer than the ones worn by men.

Cloaks worn by people of the highest rank were considered treasures, or **taonga**. They were even given their own names. In one gift exchange in the 1800's, a chief exchanged a cloak named Karamaene for a famous war canoe.

THE FEATHER CLOAK

The feather cloak was—and is—one of the most precious Maori possessions. Feather cloaks were often made with feathers from the wood pigeon or the kaka, a kind of parrot. The most prized cloaks were made from white kiwi feathers. Cloaks made from the huia bird (now **extinct**) also had great value. The feathers were woven into the flax fabric, either one by one or in small bunches.

Body Paint, Hairstyles, and Jewelry

Maori liked to **adorn** themselves in other ways. They painted their faces and bodies with a mixture of red coloring and shark liver oil. Maori men of high rank let their hair grow long. The hair would then be oiled, braided, and gathered into a topknot. This topknot was decorated with feathers and a comb of wood or bone.

Free people of low rank wore **ornaments** made from shells or birds' wings. People of higher rank wore necklaces and bracelets of bone and ivory beads. They also wore **pendants** made from greenstone, whales' teeth, and other precious materials.

▼ A print of a Maori warrior and his wife from the early 1700's. The man wears his hair in a topknot with feathers; the woman's hair is braided.

Hunting, Fishing, and Farming

Catching, gathering, growing, and preparing food were year-round activities for Maori. Crops such as **kumara** were planted in October, which was springtime in New Zealand. Harvest started in February, when summer was nearing its end. Autumn—from March through May—was the prime eel-catching season. Hunters trapped rats and birds during late fall and winter, from May to September.

◀ The skull and neck of a moa, extraordinarily well preserved in the dry atmosphere of a cave. Although these large flightless birds once provided a plentiful source of food, they became **extinct**, probably because of excessive hunting and the destruction of their lowland forest habitat by early Maori settlers.

In Search of the Moa

The moa was one of the largest birds that ever lived. The biggest species (kinds) of moa measured about 6 feet (2 meters) tall at the top of their back. Their heads may have reached as high as 10 to 13 feet (3 to 4 meters). They weighed as much as 500 pounds (225 kilograms). The huge birds could run fast. But they were wingless and so could not fly. As a result, they were easy to hunt. The meat from a single moa could feed at least 50 Maori for a day.

Changes in Diet

The Polynesians who first settled in **Aotearoa** brought dogs, which were raised for their skins, fur, and meat, and were probably also used for hunting. Rats came too, perhaps as stowaways. The rats thrived in the wild and were trapped for food.

Polynesians elsewhere also raised chickens and pigs, a great favorite. But Maori did not have them in New Zealand. Possibly they did not survive the long canoe trip across the Pacific. Or they may have been ill-suited to the colder New Zealand climate.

A Land of Plenty

Early Polynesians found plenty to eat in Aotearoa. Fur seals and large moa *(MOH uh)* birds were easy prey. In fact, moa were too easy to hunt—Maori hunters killed so many birds that they completely died out. Large numbers of seals were also hunted. Maori preserved the meat in airtight containers made from hollowed-out **gourds**.

When the easy-to-find meat was gone, Maori had other choices. They snared wood pigeons and bush parrots. Dogs were used to hunt kiwi and kakapo. Bird calls helped to attract wood hens, which hunters then snagged with a noose on the end of a stick. Women gathered shellfish. Men used lines and hooks to catch small varieties of shark and skate. Eels were plentiful in New Zealand rivers.

Maori also gathered wild plants. Forests yielded fruits and berries. One of the most important forest foods was fern root. The roots could be gathered, pounded into flour, and used in flat cakes. Slaves and others of low rank were given raw fern root.

▼ Maori women cook food by putting it in bags, then suspending the bags in the boiling water of a hot spring.

EDUCATION AND LANGUAGE

Grandparents and parents were a Maori child's main teachers. Through stories and songs, grandparents taught their grandchildren about Maori history and their ancestors. As children grew older, they learned basic skills from their parents and other **clan** members.

From an early age, children also learned Maori beliefs and **rituals**. They attended gatherings and ceremonies on the **marae**. Because **tapu** affected many areas of daily life, respect for this belief was a major part of early childhood education.

▲ Modern Maori children enjoy an outdoor lesson at Waima School, outside the mainly Maori village of Waima, on the North Island.

Maori arts were also an important source of knowledge. Each carving, weave pattern, and **taonga** had its particular history and tradition.

The Maori Language

The Maori language had much in common with languages spoken by other peoples from eastern Polynesia. Tribes and clans that lived in different parts of New Zealand spoke the language in slightly different ways. These variations of the language are known as **dialects**. Three main dialects of Maori developed—Eastern North Island, Western North Island, and South Island.

Before the Europeans came, Maori had no written language. Knowledge was passed down from generation to generation through the spoken word. Speaking well was viewed as a great skill.

Advanced Education

As children grew older, their education became more advanced. Someone who showed skill in a particular area—for example, healing or tattooing—would be trained as an expert, or **tohunga**. Knowledge and experience were gained by working alongside someone who was already a tohunga.

Students with good minds and excellent memories attended a special school run by priests. There, during the winter, small groups of students learned about Maori history, rituals, and gods.

▶ A wooden comb, which would have been worn in a man's topknot. Combs were tapu, or set apart, as were all things worn on the head. Such objects were kept safely in boxes, where they would not be handled by anyone who was unqualified to touch them. Maori children spent a great deal of time learning which objects and activities were tapu.

SPEAK MAORI!
Here are a few common Maori words and phrases:

Te reo Maori (teh reh oh mow ree)
The Maori language

Kia ora! (kee aw rah)
Hi!

Haere mai (hy ray my)
Welcome!

Tama (tah mah)
Son

Tamahine (tah mah hee nay)
Daughter

Tane (tah nay)
Man, husband

Wahine (wuh hee nay)
Woman, wife

Kaumatua (kow mah too ah)
Elders

E noho ra (ay noh hoh rah)
Goodbye (said by the person leaving)

SPORTS AND GAMES

Maori children played with kites and toy boats made from **flax** fiber. Another favorite toy was the **poi** ball. The poi was woven from flax, stuffed, decorated with shells, and attached to a cord. Girls did a dance in which they twirled the poi ball to keep their hands flexible for weaving. Boys also used the poi to build up strength in their hands and arms for fighting and hunting. Swimming was also a popular pastime.

Children—mostly boys—developed their fighting skills using flax flower stalks in place of clubs. Practice with the flower stalk of the toetoe, a wild grass, helped young Maori learn how to use darts and spears.

Adults also played games and sports, especially after the autumn harvest was finished. They competed in wrestling, flying kites, throwing darts, and spinning tops.

▲ A child's carved wooden toboggan. Maori children enjoyed sliding down steep hills on wood planks or on leaves.

Kite Traditions

Kites were not just for fun. A kite could be used to signal another village—for example, to send a message that someone had died. Kites were also used as a way to find out whether the gods favored a particular course of action. One kind of kite flown by priests was so heavy it took several people to control it.

Maori used the same word for kite as for bird—*manu*. Another name for a kite was *pakau (pah kah oo)*, which means *a bird's wing*.

▲ A girl plays a traditional string game while her friend looks on. Both girls are wearing flax cloaks and feathers in their hair.

ATTACK OF THE KITE MAN!

One Maori **legend** tells of a chief named Nukupewapewa *(noo koo peh wah peh wah)*. In the 1800's, he launched a war against an enemy **pa.** The pa was located at the foot of a cliff. The chief tried many tactics to reach the pa, but each attack failed. Finally, the chief had his warriors build a kite shaped like a large bird. In the dark of night, one of the warriors—perhaps Nukupewapewa himself—was strapped to the kite. He jumped off the cliff and floated down into the village below. Quickly he opened the gates of the pa, and the other warriors were able to storm inside.

Different Kinds of Kites

Kites flown by young children were made in such simple shapes as triangles and rectangles. Kites used for other purposes were more complex. Some were shaped and decorated to look like birds. A large bird kite was the manu kahu, named for the kahu, a New Zealand hawk that looked like a parrot. One surviving manu kahu measures nearly 12 feet (3.7 meters) across. Another kind of kite was the manu totoriwai, which resembled a robin. This kite, usually reserved for men of high rank, required special skill to build and fly.

Kites also resembled other creatures, such as fish. One surviving kite has the face and body of a man but wings like a bird. This bird-man kite even has a mask with teeth and a **moko.**

MUSIC AND DANCE

By far the best-known form of Maori music and dance was the **haka**. A Maori **legend** says that the first chief to use a haka was named Tinirau. When Tinirau learned that his pet whale had been killed by a priest named Kae, the chief sent out a group of women to find him. They did not know what Kae looked like, but they had heard he had crooked teeth. The women came to Kae's village and did the haka. When the men in the village witnessed the haka, they smiled and gazed in wonder. The women spotted Kae's terrible teeth and captured him right away.

The war chant was the most impressive type of haka. It called on Tu, the god of war, and warned enemy fighters how the attackers were going to destroy them.

Experiencing the Haka

The dance that accompanied the war haka was designed to terrify the enemy. The dancers—women as well as men—stamped and roared, slapped their bodies, bulged out their eyes, and stuck out their tongues.

Every part of the body was used in the haka—eyes, tongue, arms, hands, feet, legs, and voice. One haka began with this shout:

Slap the hands against the thighs
Puff out the chest
Bend the knees
Let the hip follow
Stamp the feet as hard as you can.

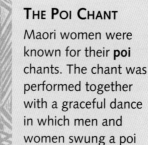

THE POI CHANT
Maori women were known for their **poi** chants. The chant was performed together with a graceful dance in which men and women swung a poi ball around their bodies. Today, this dance is performed only by women.

◀ A beautifully carved wooden Maori musical instrument, dating from the 1800's or 1900's, could be played in two ways. Musicians could blow into it like a trumpet. They could also play it like a flute by blowing across the top. Maori used such flute trumpets to signal that a chief was returning to the village as well as to accompany chants.

▲ Present-day Maori men perform a traditional war haka.

Other Kinds of Music

Maori music included much more than haka. Songs, chants, and dances were an important part of the welcoming ceremony, or **powhiri**. Maori also used music to soothe people suffering from illness and to ease the pain of getting a **moko**.

Maori made flutes from shells, wood, bird bones—even from human bones. A propeller-shaped slab of wood, attached to a cord and spun rapidly through the air, made a loud moaning sound. Large roots became horns, and **conch** *(kongk or konch)* shells were turned into trumpets. Maori instruments were often decorated with the image of Hineraukatauri *(hee neh rah oo kah tah oo ree)*, the goddess of music.

MAORI AND PAKEHA

The first Europeans known to have reached New Zealand arrived in the 1600's. By this time, Polynesians had been living in the land they called **Aotearoa** for about 400 years. The Europeans sailed under the flags of different countries, but Maori called them by a single name—**Pakeha**.

First Contact

On Dec. 13, 1642, a Dutch navigator named Abel Janszoon Tasman *(AH buhl YAHN sohn TAZ muhn)* sighted the west coast of the South Island. He sailed northward and dropped anchor five days later in a large bay at the South Island's northern tip. Tasman's crew and Maori canoeists exchanged shouts and trumpet blasts.

The following day's encounter was worse. A Maori war canoe approached Tasman's vessel. Tasman described the warriors as "of ordinary height but rough in voice and bones, their color between brown and yellow." Their hair was black, and their topknots were adorned with feathers.

Other Maori canoes appeared, and one rammed a small boat the Dutch sent out to meet them. In the fighting that followed, four European sailors were killed. The sailors fired on the Maori canoes with cannon and **muskets.** Tasman pulled up anchor and sped northward, never to return. His view of the Maori was summed up in the name he gave the harbor—Murderers' Bay. (It was renamed Golden Bay in the 1800's.)

▼ A portrait of the Dutch explorer Abel Janszoon Tasman (1603–1659), painted in the 1600's.

▶ A painted Maori war canoe paddle collected by Captain Cook on the east coast of the North Island in 1769.

The Voyages of Captain Cook

More than 120 years passed before the next contact between Maori and Pakeha. On Oct. 6, 1769, a 12-year-old boy named Nicholas Young, sailing on the H.M.S. *Endeavour* with Captain James Cook, caught sight of the North Island. Soon after, the *Endeavour* anchored at Poverty Bay, near what is now the district of Gisborne.

Cook's relations with Maori started almost as badly as Tasman's. When Cook and the scientist Joseph Banks came ashore, they got into a fight with a group of Maori warriors, killing two and wounding several others. Over time, however, Cook developed genuine respect for New Zealand's original people.

Cook made three voyages to New Zealand, spending more than 320 days there. He tried to treat people fairly and punished crew members who stole from Maori. But he left no doubt that New Zealand was ripe for European settlement. Maori would no longer have the islands to themselves.

"TUPAIA'S SHIP"

Sailing with Captain Cook was a crew member named Tupaia. Tupaia was a priest from Tahiti, an island in the Pacific. As a Polynesian, Tupaia spoke a language similar to Maori. He was able to translate between Maori and the Pakeha. Maori thought of him as the most important crewman, and they thought of the *Endeavour* as "Tupaia's ship."

THE TREATY OF WAITANGI

As more Europeans arrived, relations between Maori and **Pakeha** became extremely complicated. Some Maori resisted and attacked the European newcomers. Others cooperated with the Pakeha.

The Maori way of life changed in ways both large and small. Traditional religious beliefs faded under the influence of Christian **missionaries.** Some Maori left their villages to work on Pakeha whaling vessels. Others made money in the timber trade. Pigs and white potatoes were brought in from Australia, altering the Maori diet.

One of the biggest changes was in Maori warfare. **Muskets** bought or traded from the Pakeha replaced clubs and spears as weapons of choice. **Haka** chants and dances could not strike fear into the hearts of enemies who had guns.

Signing the Treaty of Waitangi

Before 1840, there was no clear way to settle disputes peacefully between Maori and Pakeha, or between one Maori tribe and another. The British government wanted to end this confusion and also

BRIEF TIMELINE OF MAORI AND NEW ZEALAND HISTORY	
About 1200	First Polynesians begin arriving in **Aotearoa**
1642	Voyage of Abel Janszoon Tasman
1769	First voyage of Captain James Cook
1840	Treaty of Waitangi
1863	A law allows land to be seized from Maori rebels
1975	Maori protest march; Waitangi Tribunal formed
1987	Maori becomes an official language of New Zealand

to regulate the behavior of European settlers, who were renowned for their lawlessness and drunkenness. Britain decided to turn New Zealand into a **colony.** This meant New Zealand would be subject to British rule and British law. The British sent a naval officer, William Hobson, to New Zealand. He was told to make a treaty with Maori.

◀ A hand-colored print by George French Angas shows three Maori chiefs of the 1800's. On the left is Te Wherowhero, chief of Waikato. He refused to sign the 1840 Treaty of Waitangi, in which the Maori gave sovereignty (control) of their lands to the British government.

▲ The Treaty of Waitangi was signed in 1840 in the house built for British official James Busby on the Bay of Islands, North Island. Busby was one of the authors of the treaty. In 1835, Busby had helped more than 30 Maori chiefs draft the Declaration of Independence of New Zealand. This document proclaimed the country's independence and attempted to create a national Maori government.

On Feb. 5, 1840, Hobson met with an assembly of Maori chiefs at Waitangi *(WY tuhng ee or WY tahng ee)*, on the North Island. Some chiefs opposed the treaty because they distrusted the Pakeha. But on February 6, more than 40 chiefs agreed to the treaty. Other chiefs added their names later. This meant New Zealand would be subject to British rule and British law, and individuals or private companies would be unable to purchase land without the approval of the British government.

After Waitangi

The Treaty of Waitangi solved some problems but created others. For one thing, the Maori chiefs and the British governors understood the treaty in different ways. Maori thought they still had some power over their lands. The British, on the other hand, thought they had become the sole rulers of New Zealand. Maori still owned property, but according to the treaty, Pakeha settlers were able to purchase that property from the British government without Maori approval or knowledge.

Soon the settlers began demanding more land. Disputes with Maori erupted into open warfare. Maori tried to halt land sales to the Pakeha. But in 1863, the government passed a new law that allowed it to take land from Maori who had been declared rebels. Millions of acres were seized from Maori. They lost the war—and their lands.

DECLINE AND REVIVAL

KEEPING THE MAORI LANGUAGE ALIVE

Sir James Henare was an important Maori leader and teacher. He fought fearlessly in World War II (1939–1945). Later he recalled how, when he was growing up, many Pakeha school officials had tried to force young Maori to give up their language and culture. "English is the bread-and-butter language," he was told. "And if you want to earn your bread and butter you must speak English." A school official ordered Henare to cut down a stem of the supplejack bush and then beat him with it for speaking Maori in school. As an adult, Henare helped to revive Maori education.

In 1858, New Zealand had about 56,400 Maori and 59,400 Pakeha. By 1901, the number of Pakeha had increased to 770,300, while the number of Maori had fallen to 45,500. Wars and disease had contributed to the Maori decline. By the end of the 1800's, Maori were losing their lands, their language, their culture, and their future.

New Leaders, New Hope

In the early 1900's, a new generation of leaders began to revive Maori culture. One of those leaders was Sir Apirana Turupa Ngata *(ah pee rah nah too roo pah ngah tah)*. Ngata had both Pakeha and Maori ancestors. He had grown up speaking the Maori language, but he went to Pakeha schools. He was the first Maori to earn a degree from a New Zealand university.

Trained as a lawyer, he held several high government posts. But his influence went much deeper. He helped to revive Maori ties with the land. He was an excellent performer of **haka**. He also encouraged other traditional arts, including **poi** dancing, woodcarving, and kite making.

▶ Maori girls at a British-style school in Auckland in the early 1900's.

▲ A Maori woodcarver shares his skills in front of his home in Rotorua, on the North Island, in the early 1900's. A return to traditional crafts played a big part in reviving Maori culture.

Another influential Maori leader was Te Puea Herangi *(teh poo eh ah heh rang ee)*. She was the granddaughter of a king, and she devoted her life to helping Maori regain some of the land and power that British rulers had taken from them in the 1860's. She also helped Ngata in his efforts to revive Maori arts.

Social Changes

Meanwhile, major social changes were taking place within Maori society. Health and living conditions had begun to improve. Maori fought alongside other New Zealanders in World War I (1914–1918), winning the respect of Pakeha troops. Maori and Pakeha troops also played an important role in World War II (1939–1945), assisting the United Kingdom and the United States.

After World War II, many Maori began leaving their villages. By the 1960's, for the first time, about 60 percent of Maori lived in cities.

TRADITION AND CHANGE

Today, many Maori have had great success in the **Pakeha** world. Kiri Te Kanawa, who has both Maori and Pakeha ancestors, is a renowned opera singer. She also has recorded traditional Maori music. Keisha Castle-Hughes, who is part Maori, starred in the 2002 movie *Whale Rider*. She was only 13 years old when she was nominated for an Academy Award as best actress. Well-known artist Cliff Whiting often uses Maori **myths** and **legends** in his work.

Protest and Reform

In the 1970's, many Maori embraced the idea that **Aotearoa**/New Zealand was one country with two great peoples and traditions. They claimed the Pakeha had treated Maori unfairly and stolen their land. In 1975, Maori protesters held a huge march. They walked from the northern end of North Island to the capital city of Wellington—a distance of about 400 miles (640 kilometers).

The march had a major effect on New Zealand. Government officials set up a tribunal of Maori and Pakeha officials to hear and attempt

▲ Dame Kiri Te Kanawa, who has Maori ancestors, is one of the world's greatest opera singers.

◀ Maori activists protest at Waitangi Day celebrations, held to mark the signing of the 1840 Treaty of Waitangi. Activists argue that those Europeans who took Maori land did not honor the terms of the treaty.

▲ Maori **poi** dancers perform at Waitangi Day celebrations.

to settle disputes about Maori land. At first, the tribunal discussed only recent complaints. But in 1985, it gained the power to deal with land claims dating back to the signing of the Treaty of Waitangi in 1840.

Maori Prospects

In the 1990's and early 2000's, the tribunal settled several major tribal land claims. In 1995, the British government formally apologized for its treatment of Maori. In June 2008, the New Zealand government and seven Maori tribes signed a historic agreement. It transferred ownership of 435,000 acres (176,000 hectares) of forest plantations and forest rents worth $319 million to about 100,000 people of Maori descent.

Maori still face problems. Many have a hard time finding a job or good health care. Despite these concerns, Maori today have a brighter future than anyone thought possible 100 years ago. One of every seven people living in New Zealand claims Maori ancestry. Maori culture is thriving. Maori children have the right to attend classes in Maori, English, or both. Radio and television stations broadcast in the Maori language. And that language— *Te reo Maori*—has been declared a treasure, or **taonga**, that all New Zealanders must protect.

GLOSSARY

adorn Decorate.

adz A hand tool resembling an ax, used to chop, shape, and smooth wood.

Aotearoa The Maori name for New Zealand. It translates to *the land of the long white cloud.*

archaeologist A scientist who studies the remains of past human cultures.

ariki A paramount chief.

clan A group of people who are related through a common ancestor.

colony A territory inhabited by people who leave their own country and settle in another land; the territory is usually distant from the country that governs it.

conch A large spiral sea shell.

dialect A variation in a language used by a particular group of people.

DNA A substance that controls the formation, growth, and reproduction of every living cell. The full name for DNA is deoxyribonucleic acid.

elder An older and more influential member of a tribe or community.

extinct Died out completely.

flax A plant raised for its fiber and seed. Its fiber can be made into rope, fabric, and many other products.

fortified Protected against attack.

gourd A vegetable that is closely related to the pumpkin and squash.

haka A Maori chant and dance.

hapu A group of people who are related through a common ancestor; **clan.**

Hawaiki The legendary land from which Polynesians believe their ancestors came.

hongi A traditional Maori greeting in which one person presses his or her nose against the nose of a guest.

hull The body or frame of a canoe, boat, or ship.

iwi A Maori tribe or tribes.

jade A hard, tough, and highly colored stone. Jade comes in a wide range of colors, including dark green, white, yellow, gray, red, and black.

kainga A Maori village that is not **fortified** with fences.

kete A basket or baskets.

kumara A kind of sweet potato.

legend A folk story, often set in the past, which may be based in truth, but which may also contain fictional or fantastic elements. Legends are similar to myths, but myths often are about such sacred topics as gods or the creation of the world.

mana Supernatural power or influence that flows through objects, persons, or places.

marae An open-air meeting place found in many Polynesian villages.

mauri Life force.

midden A refuse heap.

migrate To move from one place to another.

missionary A person who works to spread a religion.

moko A tattoo.

muru The right to get revenge by taking someone else's property.

musket A long, heavy, shoulder-fired gun introduced in the 1500's and widely used before the development of the rifle.

myth See **legend.**

navigate To sail, manage, or steer a boat on a course or to a destination.

noa Ordinary; commonplace (the opposite of **tapu**).

ornament A decorative accessory.

pa A **fortified** Maori village.

Pakeha People of non-Maori ancestry.

pendant A hanging body **ornament.**

poi A ball woven from **flax** fiber.

powhiri A Maori ceremony of welcome.

prow The pointed front part of a ship or boat.

rangatira The leader of a **hapu.**

ritual A solemn or important act or ceremony, often religious in nature.

sacred Holy.

supernatural Above or beyond what is natural.

ta moko The art of tattooing.

tangihanga A funeral.

taonga A treasured possession.

tapu Special; set apart; sacred (the opposite of **noa**).

tiki A carved image of a Polynesian god or ancestor.

tohunga An expert; a person with special skills.

utu The idea of balance in social relations.

whakapapa The Maori word for ancestors.

whanau An extended family.

whare whakairo A carved meeting house.

ADDITIONAL RESOURCES

Books

Introducing Maori Art
by Deidre Brown (Reed Publishing, 2005)

Land of the Long White Cloud: Maori Myths, Tales, and Legends
by Kiri Te Kanawa (Pavilion Books, 1997)

Maori
by Robert MacDonald (Thomson Learning, 1994)

The Maori of New Zealand
by Steve Theunissen (Lerner Publications, 2003)

New Zealand: Land of the Long White Cloud
by Valerie Keyworth (Dillon Press, 1999)

Reed Book of Maori Exploration
by A. W. Reed and Ross Calman
(Reed Publishing, 2006)

Reed Book of Maori Mythology
by A. W. Reed and Ross Calman
(Reed Publishing, 2004)

Ta Moko: The Art of Maori Tattoo
by D. R. Simmons (Reed Publishing, 1997)

The Whale Rider
by Witi Tame Ihimaera (Harcourt, 2003)

Web Sites

http://www.aucklandmuseum.com/5/maori-culture

http://www.newzealand.com/travel/about-nz/culture/culture-maori-culture.cfm

http://www.newzealand.com/travel/app_templates/haka/index_content.html

http://www.nzhistory.net.nz/category/tid/133

http://www.nzhistory.net.nz/culture/maori-language-week/100-maori-words

http://www.nzhistory.net.nz/war/new-zealands-19th-century-wars/introduction

http://www.tamuseum.org.nz/uploads/23778/index.html

http://www.teara.govt.nz/en/maori-new-zealanders

INDEX

Acknowledgments

Alexander Turnbull Library/National Library of New Zealand: 22, 25, 49, 54; The Art Archive: 4 (Stephanie Colasanti), 7; Bridgeman Art Library: 12 (Auckland City Art Gallery), 17, 52, 56; Corbis: 15, 18 (Bettmann), 19 (Reuters), 30 (Bettmann), 34 (George Steinmetz), 37 (Macduff Everton), 38 (Bettmann), 43 (Historical Picture Archive), 45(Bettmann), 46 (Paul A. Souders), 51 (Anders Ryman), 55 (Nik Wheeler), 57 (Bettmann), 58b (Paul A. Souders), 58t (Hulton-Deutsch Collection), 59 (Paul A. Souders); The Kobal Collection: 13 (New Zealand Film Commission); Shutterstock: 5 (Colin and Linda McKie); Werner Forman Archive: 1 (Entwistle Gallery, London), 6, 9, 10 (National Museum of New Zealand), 11 (Auckland Institute and Museum), 14, 16 (British Museum), 20 (Otago Museum, Dunedin), 21 (Entwistle Gallery, London), 23 (Auckland Institute and Museum), 26 (Entwistle Gallery, London), 27 (National Museum of New Zealand), 28, 29 (Auckland Institute and Museum), 31 (National Museum of New Zealand), 32 (Canterbury Museum, Christchurch), 33 (Entwistle Gallery, London), 35 (British Museum), 36 (National Museum of New Zealand), 39 (Auckland Institute and Museum), 40, 42 (Canterbury Museum, Christchurch), 44 (National Museum of New Zealand), 47 (National Museum of New Zealand), 48 (Auckland Institute and Museum), 50 (British Museum), 53 (British Museum).

Cover image: Werner Forman Archive (Otago Museum, Dunedin)
Back cover image: Shutterstock (Joop Snijder, Jr.)